Holidays

Christmas

by Rebecca Pettiford

Bullfrog Books

Ideas for Parents and Teachers

Bullfrog Books let children practice reading informational text at the earliest reading levels. Repetition, familiar words, and photo labels support early readers.

Before Reading

• Discuss the cover photo. What does it tell them?

• Look at the picture glossary together. Read and discuss the words.

Read the Book

• "Walk" through the book and look at the photos. Let the child ask questions. Point out the photo labels.

• Read the book to the child, or have him or her read independently.

After Reading

• Prompt the child to think more. Ask: Does your family celebrate Christmas? What sorts of things do you see around Christmastime?

Bullfrog Books are published by Jump!
5357 Penn Avenue South
Minneapolis, MN 55419
www.jumplibrary.com

Library of Congress Cataloging-in-Publication Data
Pettiford, Rebecca.
  Christmas / by Rebecca Pettiford.
     pages cm.—(Holidays)
  Includes bibliographical references and index.
  Summary: "This photo-illustrated book for early readers describes the Christian holiday of Christmas and the things people do to celebrate it."
Provided by publisher.
  Audience: Ages 5-8.
  Audience: Grade K to 3.
  ISBN 978-1-62031-128-8 (hardcover)
  ISBN 978-1-62496-195-3 (ebook)
  1. Christmas—Juvenile literature. I. Title.
  GT4985.5.P48 2015
  394.2663--dc23

                      2013046804

Editor: Wendy Dieker
Series Designer: Ellen Huber
Book Designer: Lindaanne Donohoe
Photo Researcher: Kurtis Kinneman

Photo Credits: All photos by Shutterstock except: Blend Images/SuperStock, 16–17; Chuck Savage/ Corbis, 18–19, 23tl; Dreamstime.com, 9; Imagebroker/ Dr. Wilfried Bahnmüller/Alamy, 8–9; iStock, 14; JLP/Jose L. Pelaez/Corbis, 20–21; Charles Taylor/ Shutterstock.com, 21

Printed in the United States of America at Corporate Graphics in North Mankato, Minnesota.
3-2014
10 9 8 7 6 5 4 3 2 1

Table of Contents

What Is Christmas?

Christmas is a Christian holiday.

It is December 25.

What do Christians celebrate?

The birth of Jesus.

They call him the Son of God.

baby
Jesus

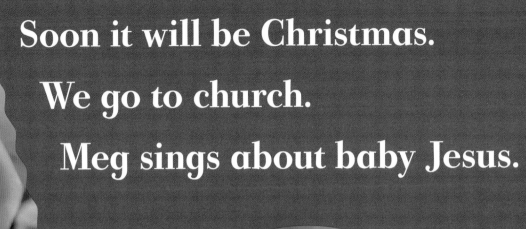

Soon it will be Christmas.

We go to church.

Meg sings about baby Jesus.

We shop.
We buy gifts.

Look! It's Santa!

Dan asks him for a bike.

11

We put up a Christmas tree.

We hang the lights.

Tia hangs the ornaments.

lights

We wrap gifts.
Zoe helps Mom.

14

To **Dad**

From **Zoe**

15

We make
cookies. Yum!

Bella and Sam
frost them. Pretty!

Ding-dong!
Who's at the door?
Carolers!
They sing songs.

It's Christmas day.
Ben gets a gift.
It's a toy car.
Merry Christmas!

Symbols of Christmas

Christmas tree

Santa

baby Jesus

gifts

Picture Glossary

carolers
A group of people who visits others and sings Christmas songs for them.

Jesus
The man Christians believe is the Son of God; also called Jesus Christ.

Christian
A person who believes that Jesus is the Son of God and follows his teachings as written in the Bible.

ornaments
Objects that make something look pretty.

Index

To Learn More

Learning more is as easy as 1, 2, 3.

1) Go to www.factsurfer.com

2) Enter "Christmas" into the search box.

3) Click the "Surf" button to see a list of websites.

With factsurfer.com, finding more information is just a click away.